FIRSTMATTERPRESS

Portland, Ore.

EVEN THE AIR, TOO HEAVY

EVEN THE AIR, TOO HEAVY

riley danvers

FIRSTMATTERPRESS

Portland, Ore.

First Edition

Published in the United States
by First Matter Press
Portland, Oregon

Paperback ISBN 978-1-958600-01-6

Lead Editors: Edited by Caroline Wilcox Reul & Emily Moon
Contributing Editors: Ash Good, Lauren Paredes
& Natalie Garyet

First Matter Press Cohort Collaborators:
Xylophone Mykland, Hailey Spencer,
Sonya Wohletz & ahuva s. zaslavsky

Cover Cyanotype: *Heart in Your Throat*
Copyright © 2022 by Rachel Mulder
rchlmldr.com

Book Design: Ash Good
ashgood.com

This book is dedicated to my late grandmother,
Orpha Caton.
I miss you every single day.
Thank you for inspiring me to write poetry.

POEMS

"This ink. This name. This blood
and wonder. This box. This body in a box. This blood
in the body. This wind in the blood."
—Terrance Hayes, *Wind in a Box*

"The widening line that splits
your body into halves
was always a starmap
to home."
—Vanessa Angelica Villarreal, *Beast Meridian*

KALEIDOSCOPE

I strain my eyes across this ocean, peel
back time to remember when I
contained cherry air, before

you gave way to the storm
that rocked your anchors, before
I housed only unmet dreams.

Because of you, I want to cling to moments
reminding me I once held more than regret.
I am always running after you.

I am deathbed and graveyard.

DISSECTED

If I cut open my abdomen
would I see your shadow?
Or would I find a hollow shape

etched in silica glass

                                        floating

in a burgundy tide?

Are fibers of tissue embedded
into my sandcastle walls,
or have I formed around your

absence?

Does my uterus remember
your turbulence?

Is your shape in my blood
a haunted mutation?

                                        Or is it
                a memory shape

                                                                shifting

                under the pull of a distant orbit?

Maybe this is how hearts
reach
for what can never be

                                reclaimed.

THROUGH THE PORES

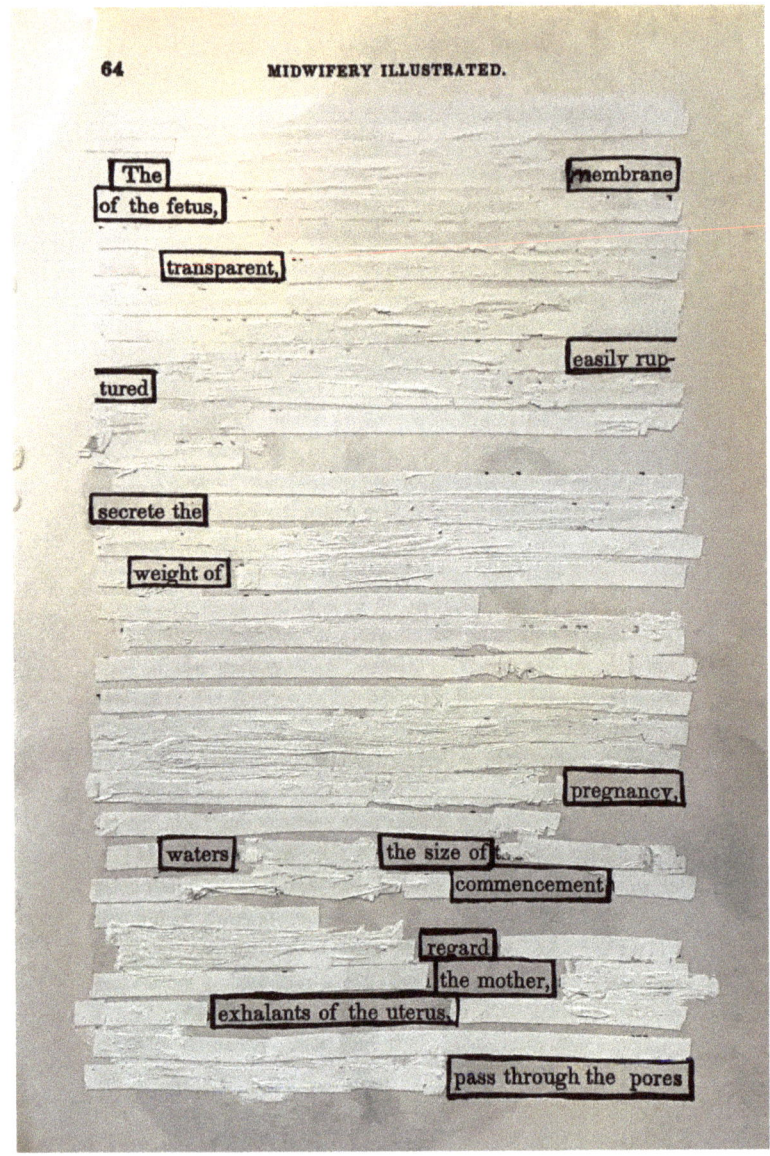

MIDWIFERY ILLUSTRATED.

The membrane
of the fetus,

transparent,

easily rup-
tured

secrete the

weight of

pregnancy,

waters   the size of
commencement

regard
the mother,
exhalants of the uterus,

pass through the pores

GRIEF

/grēf/ (noun)

1.

a.) *deep and poignant distress caused by, or as if by, bereavement:*
cold and naked on the bathroom floor, shivering and half-wet; shower
fails to calm my tempestuous body bleeding clotted golf balls, clots
that clot the shower drain; ragged iron-tanged breaths;

b.) *a cause of such suffering:* cannot go into the bathroom without
hearing the storm that pushed the fetus from my body; cannot reach
for hands never formed; cannot search for eyes never opened.

2.

a.) *trouble, annoyance:* wait every day for solitude so I can break,
allow myself to be broken; daylight keeps me hanging by fists
clenched around the ice in my throat;

b.) *annoying or playful criticism:* undo this muscle memory, undo
the aching arc, undo the shallow water of my uterus, find a wind
strong enough to carry me from this harbor;

c.) *an unfortunate outcome — disaster:* try to mend the cracks with
kinky sex, with expensive food, with whiskey and weed at night to dull
the nightmares, with hiking among mountain trees and long car rides

along rivers; try to hide the evidence, hide the stains on the floor;
try to find a future, try to write myself into a different story: there is
no heartbeat strong enough to cut through barbed wire;

d.) *mishap, misadventure:* taste pretend on my tongue like mildew;
taste smiles in my cheeks like plaster; taste disdain like mud, icicles
down my throat, piercing what little fight is left in this skin, in these
bones; taste a trail of endings like cysts of carbon and lemon zest.

BECOMING A HAVEN

My body
like a groan
can't be less
than it isn't;
a tree
or tail
or body
of scales;
the creak,
furled wings
unfurling howls.

My body
like a tree
can't move without
groaning; groans
without knowing
why; sways under
gravity of unflapped wings;
bends and arches
under starstruck tempests.
I don't like how
my body moves.

My body
moves
like groans
have grown roots
and roots have grown
wings; hot angst in bones,
the wind roams
among scales and leaves,
arcing under
beastling tracks
and forest fire.

EFFACEMENT[1] & DILATION[2]

[1] I am well acquainted
with the lathered
hiss of undead wails
with contractions crying
out for the scythe
crying out for
cloaked sails on this
tide of blood.

[2] I am less acquainted
with muscle and tissue
moving through
fields of harvested thorns
the blooming blood
of roses cut
from the stem
a bouquet of cells
undone
and pruned.

10 ANSWERS
WITHOUT QUESTIONS

I

The only sounds that live
in this tundra are all
the screams my mouth
chewed to silence.

II

I must
quiet the words
that blot themselves on the pages
of my dreams.

III

When I sleep
I wander
the cemetery of selves frozen
in search of unspoken truth.

IV

Love can
never be fully
exhumed.

V

Most days
I carry screams under my tongue
to remember I have not lost my voice.

VI

To love is to
be haunted.

VII

Sometimes love is a cage.
Sometimes the cage
is an expedition without a map.

VIII

There is no remedy
for remembering.

IX

When the bodies
buried in this landscape
thaw and awaken
ice and stone
will reveal a resurrection.

X

Winter will not last
and the moors will soon
open these graves.

DIVISION OF THE FETUS

DIVISION OF THE FETUS.

the fetus

terminated

the female
powerless

divided

belonging

backward,

formed

this difference

bones of the skull

moveable,

bones of the skull,

quadrila-
teral: the centre,

is trian-
gular,   the centre   occiput.

K

PREGNANCY
HOW-NOT-TO GUIDE

Do you know

       how   to watch a   dream   slither out

                                      of your

    body?

           To feel thorns   scratch

your   most tender   hopes?

                       Do you know how

to look

     down   at your compass   and see

       only

         the places   you've

                already been?   To

watch your coordinates

diverge

                  into thickets where
      silence and memory

   shed their skin?

FIRST PERIOD AFTER
MY SECOND MISCARRIAGE

On the floor of the bathroom
ear pressed to the door,
back spasms snake under
skin to the hollowed
and left vacant,
cramps of burnt out electric
sockets, echoes of contractions
steal away my unborn.
Body is regret.

No fetus
in my womb now,
just claws of charcoal.

Can't taste anything
now, just carbon crying
tears of phosphorous
in my bloodied
and laid-to-waste body,
my made-ruin-of
and razed-to-the-ground body.
Must recognize its silence,
eye of the storm looming,
a holding cell for unmaking.

How much death
can breathe through
my epidermis before
I too am a cloud voided
of rain?

LIKE WILDFIRE, NOW

Burnt up   bodies
are more
than   their piles of ash.

Sometimes   labor pains
are easier
than   birth

Because   death
is more familiar
than   resurrection.

KINESTHETIC ALIGNMENT[1]

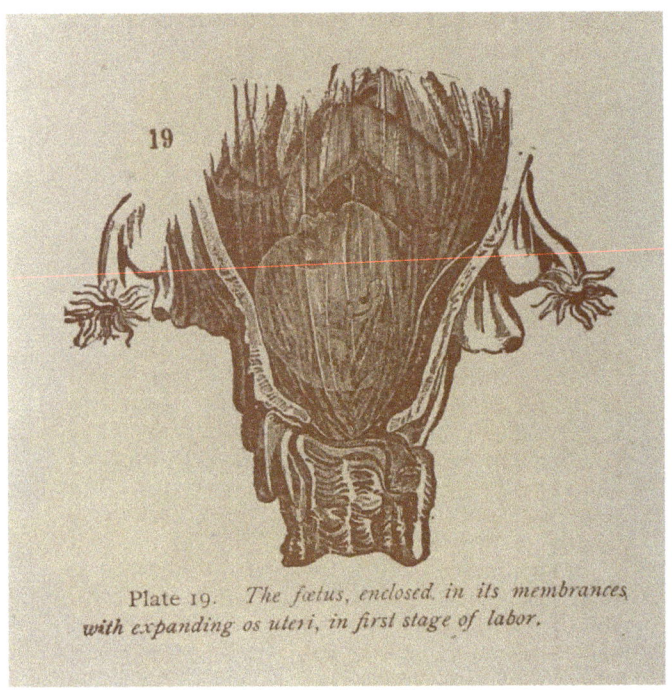

Plate 19. *The fœtus, enclosed in its membranes, with expanding os uteri, in first stage of labor.*

[1] I still feel the forgotten among waterspouts of thorns and whispers,
exhale inevitable, unviable popping of dandelions;
still feel electricity charting courses through futile chromosomes,
arcing through muscle, tissue, and bone,
lighting the sails of me ablaze,
weighing anchor in plasma-churned waters,
making my womb a watery grave;
I still feel fetal sails going limp,
letting go of wind to make a coffin.

MITOSIS

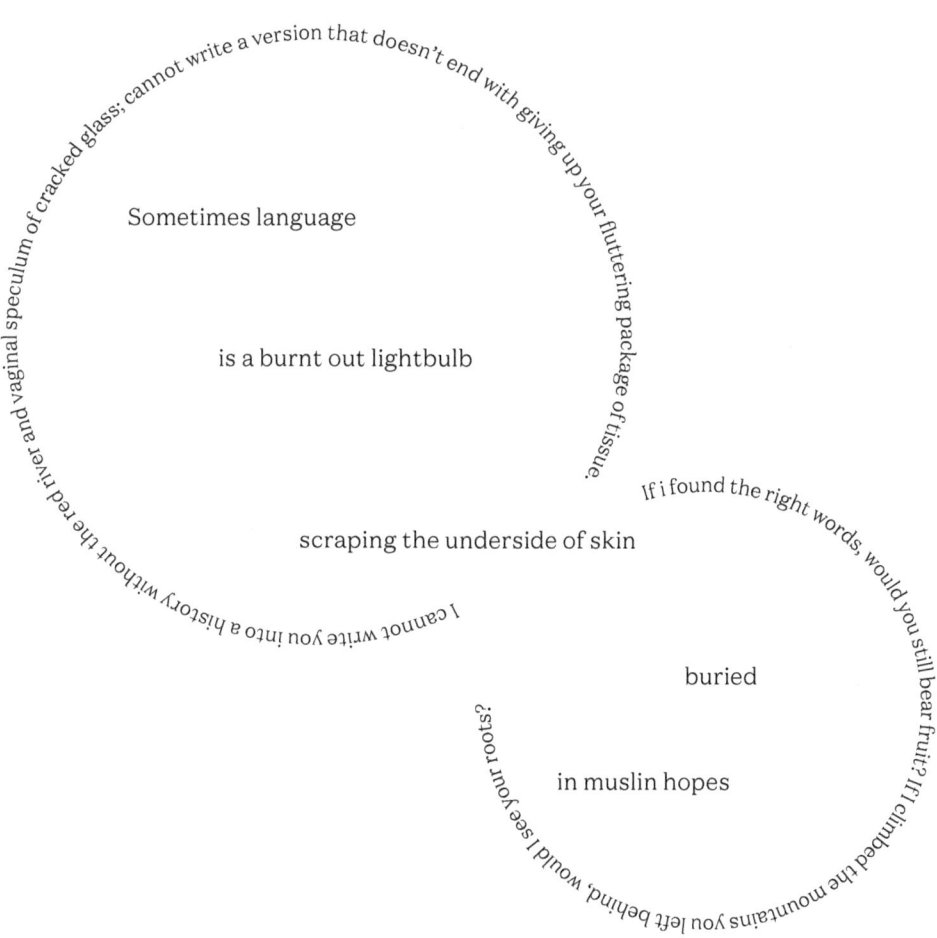

Sometimes language

is a burnt out lightbulb

scraping the underside of skin

buried

in muslin hopes

cannot write a version that doesn't end with giving up your fluttering package of tissue

I cannot write you into a history without the red river and vaginal speculum of cracked glass;

If i found the right words, would you still bear fruit? If i climbed the mountains you left behind, would I see your roots?

WHAT TO EXPECT WHEN
YOU'RE EXPECTING DEATH

I am losing
this pregnancy.
It's what my body
says must happen,
declaring mutiny
on this unborn brew
of my DNA.

Body blows open
a grief-shaped hole
in my once-birth
now-unbirth-canal.

I feel death
like
an alter ego.
My dying light
never lived.
Empty sonogram.
Blank womb.

I have no more
rage to rage with.
I cannot stop
the flow.

I CANNOT CARRY THESE FISTS

I only think of sticky
merlot clots
slithering over my sails.

I wanted to punch someone
with my balled-up fists,
but who was there to blame?

This is a memory
I do not stop reliving.

It makes me unhinge my
jaw and cry out to the moon
that stole from me.

It's a beautiful breakdown.
A toppling.

LATITUDE & LONGITUDE[1]

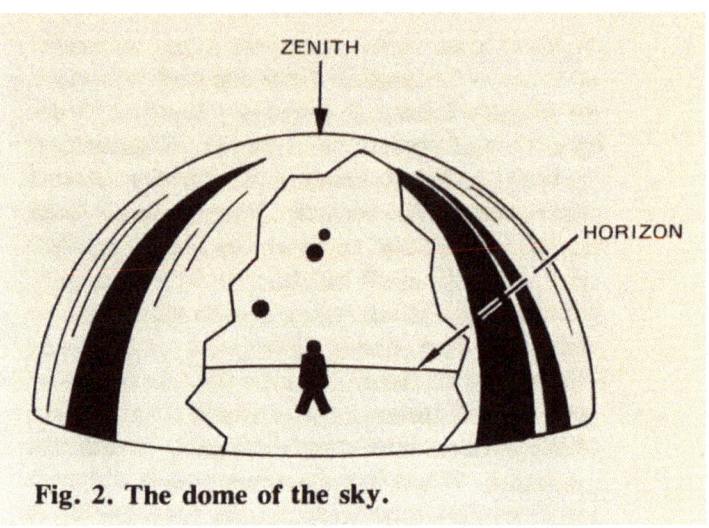

Fig. 2. The dome of the sky.

[1] If my head is the northernmost point   and toes are southernmost

     if frontface is east   and backface is west

         if flesh is made of   lines

     circling earth   then womb is the intersection

     of equator

         and prime meridian

     and there can be no other   coordinates

         to lead   me to the place

         where I have buried you.

RIVER VEINS

I want to lie down like a river
lie down in a river
lie down and become a river
because this body is static
and maybe then I'll understand
the concept of movement

I want to lie down like a river
lie down near a river
lie down and watch a river
because this body is rigid
full of mountain peaks
and maybe then I'll know
the reason for air

I want to lie down like a river
lie down close to a river
lie down and listen to a river
because there is magic and memory in water
and maybe then I'll
remember the me that emerged
from the sea

I want to lie down like a river
lie down in the woods like a river
lie down and breathe in the wind like a river

because this body aches and creaks
and maybe then I'll
hold more in my hands
than an offering of scars

I want to lie down like a river
lie down and dream of the river
lie down and merge with the river
because this body is no
longer tethered
and maybe I don't need to walk on water
to understand doubt

REMAKING

Footsteps pound
the roof of your mind,
pound the roof of
your body. Interconnected
web connecting you to
this di
        sc   on
                       ne   ct.
The pounding above
your head aches in rhythm
to the pounding of your
d
   i   s
           c   o   n
                  n   e   c   t
                           e   d
body, your   di
sjo
     i
nted joints of serenading drums.

Your body
a vessel of potential
becoming a vessel of
b   r   o   k   e   n, becoming a hull
of h o l l o w
                  and l e a k i n g.
Your body is your
un   do   ing, your
          body und   oin   g itself.
Your bathroom floor
a war zone of fetal
tissue. Body pounding fetus,
fetus pounding birth
canal, birth canal pounding
the floor with too much
of your insides for there to have
ever been life.
Pound the floor with fists
clenched like the breath you can't
release, do what you can to

dis

                         a

     ssem

                                 ble this moment
into particles you can take back into
your   b

                    r

                        o

                            k

                                e

                                    n body,

pregnancy by osmosis
because nothing is real anymore.
You are only a   mi   mi   cr y.
You want the blunt end
of a hammer to meet every part
of you that is still
no longer pregnant. Had to

d
    i
       s
         a
         s
           s
             e
               m
               b
                 l
                   e the moment

and
di
       sas
             semb
                 le

your body and now you
are filled with poundings

because you don't know how to
fill with anything else.
Your body an
        u n
        b e
        c o m
        i n g beast

becoming something new.

MONUMENT

I buried you in my body
because you had no body.
There was nothing of you
to bury. You were
never formed.

Only blood proved
you had ever been.
Only my body remains,
the last monument
of you-who-never-were.

SPONTANEOUS ABORTION[1]

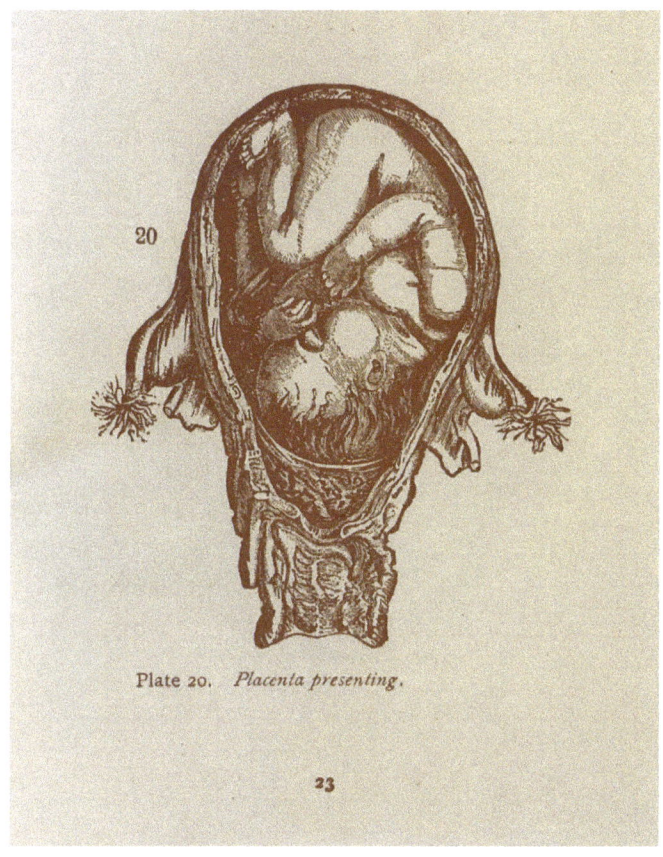

Plate 20. *Placenta presenting.*

23

[1] You lay in the afterdeath / of your first unpregnancy. You feel the fetus crawl / out of your uterus. You / look for its mangled shape among ruins.

But you / never find the body. You / tear open blood clots looking for / the piece of you / you can never repair.

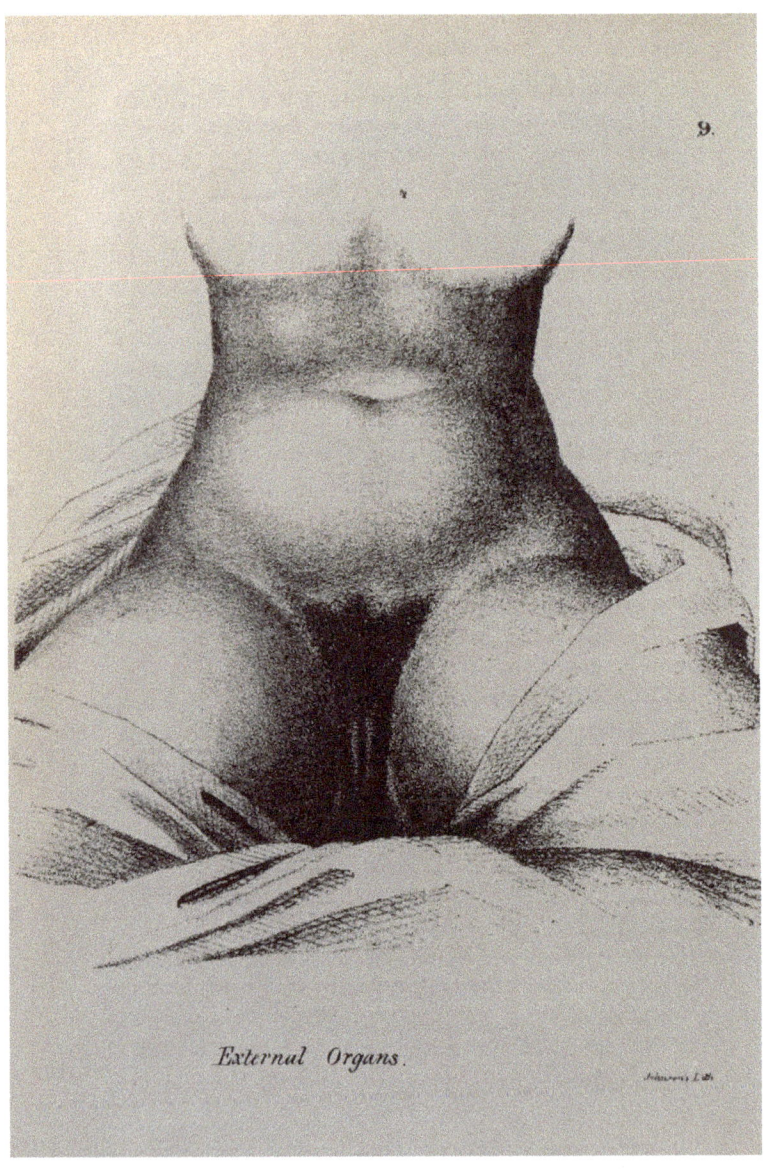

External Organs.

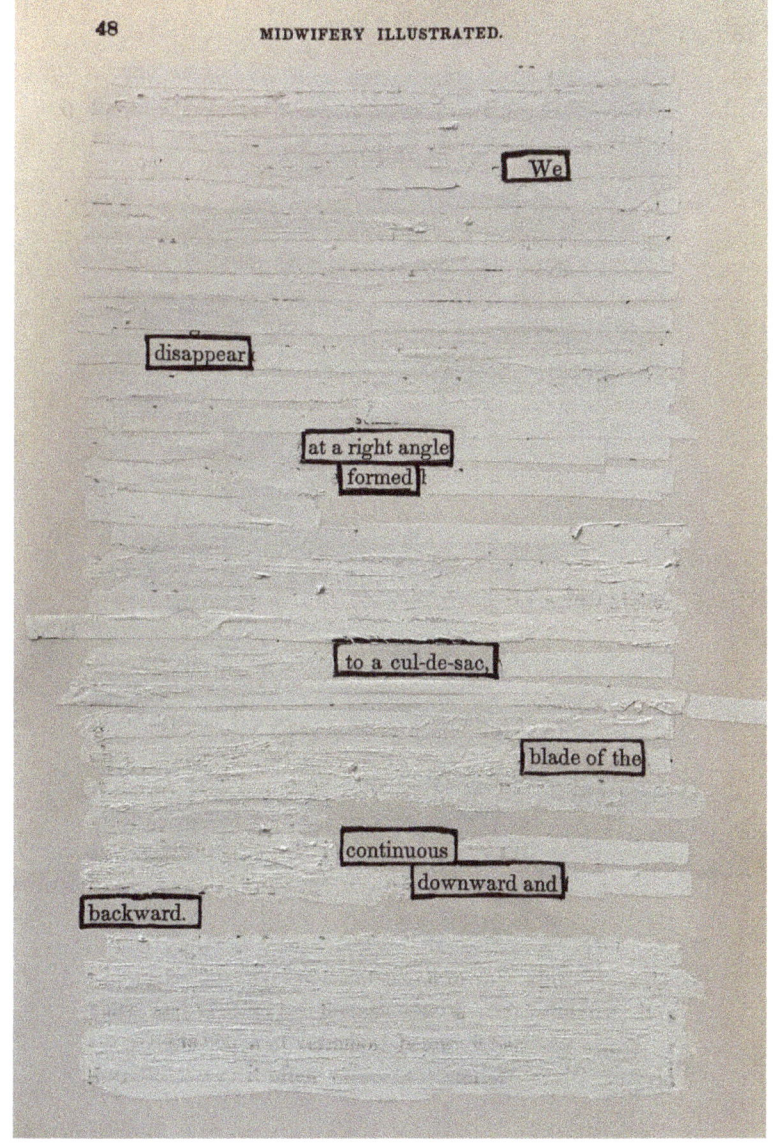

We

disappear

at a right angle
formed

to a cul-de-sac,

blade of the

continuous
downward and

backward.

BODY: LANGUAGE

right eye twitches   something   has come alive in my   body

                     died in my   body   made rapid by

                                 rumination   regret

my stationary   body   unfurls

     twitches

                too full   of wings   too full   of

fire   filling forests

               too full   of stitches   a kettle heating

water boiling   steam screaming

               stationary

      body too full

of its aching   self   body too full

                    of body   too full

       of too much

empty

I   am alive

because I   am   what has died

I   am alive

because   I

have held   what has   died

muscles   moving   in time

with time

synapses firing off   sounding

marching

jerking

twitching

switching   off

maybe   this means   I   no

            longer know

                    how to speak

                           the language of the

                living.

SWEET AND SOUR

Blood dripped down my legs in sticky clumps. Heat built in swells of wind and water. Pressure piercing into hip bones. Lightning bolts in extensors flexors obliques. Needing to urinate. Only producing a whisper that hurts to lose, whispers that hurt w orse to hold in. The painkillers did not kill my pain. I laughed as if I wasn't a destroyer, as if this pile of flesh had not uncreated what it was meant to create. I ate sweet and sour chicken. The sauce sticky and warm and red like the alm ost vacant space between my thighs. Sick and purging chicken, purging sticky sauce, purging secret cells of a mortified future. Writhing. Claws inside me, leaving marks. Screams. Pillars of shame. Death in my body like a fanned flame. And on my breath, a sulfur I had not conjured.

BUTTERFLY EFFECT

I wonder where you are in this body that used to hold you?

Cast out among snowing thorns
And wisps of crying ice   piercing cry of your
silence
No heartbeat
This is a truth

I want to rewrite

My womb
Unable to keep you   powerless to
Stop your unbecoming
This is the truth of my body

I could not stop your unbecoming

Where is somewhere-else in my body?
A clump of cells and energy waiting
I could not rewrite
This story

I want to

Rewrite your womb form
Energy does not die does not disappear
The glory of your
Unbecoming
Ripples
Nothing   is the marrow of these bones

WAYWARD WINDS[1]

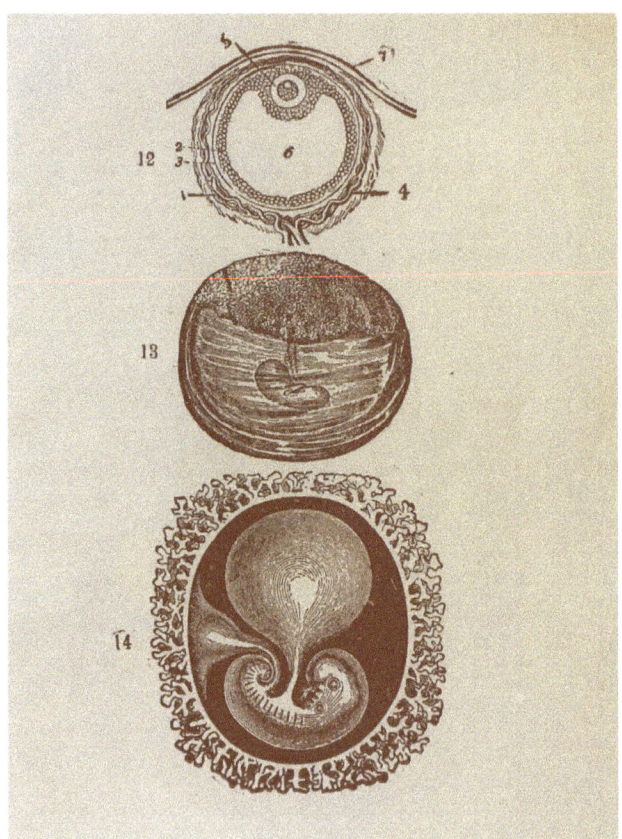

[1] **[13]** Capricious / movement inside the forest **[3]** followed the wanton, willful river **[1]** bloody, depraved **[14]** river disobeying guidance and lamplights. Current **[7]** billowed breath blowing / **[5]** neverwards **[12]** pulsing out of time.

You know you must **[6]** grow roots / of hate into your own / body. Thread your flesh **[4]** with thorns just to feel **[2]** something other than yourself.

CAPSIZING

Blood-stained wood floor.
Garbage can filled with menstrual
pads overflowed with
discarded uterine shadows.
Somewhere   the cells of a fetus.
Somewhere   the shapeless form
of an unknown future.

An emptiness more akin to
theft than loss
reaching from womb to ribs
from ribs to spleen
from spleen to nowhere.

I imagine my organs
and see piles of ash
and microscopic bones
making tumors of heartbeats
clotting veins with
breath unbreathed,
markers turning waves to tsunamis,
turning blood to cyclones of
drowning.   Turning flesh

into all I will never be able
to navigate.

DEATH HOWLER

Do you know   how

to   live   through   the death of   your own

                                                                    motherhood?

                        To watch   blood stain   skin

of your thighs   cover wood floor   of your

bathroom   spread across   the canvas

            of the life you   were building?

Do you know   how

to feel   your body   empty   itself of

            feeling? Release   last breaths

of the mother   you   might have been?

For   12 weeks   you were

              becoming someone's everything   and now your

        everything   is gone.

                                        What has become   of your

                              shape?

How   will   anything

make sense again?   14 hours   motherhood   mutates

shapeshifts   into a howl

given   up   from   your   body   given   up   to

                        moon   the only god

              listening tonight.

Crying isn't enough.   Screaming isn't enough.

Silence is
too much.

So   you

writhe   in the blood

of your   motherhood as it

falls away.

Do you know   how to thank   the earth for

silver light?   Wish

on stars   that   motherhood had

taken   you

with it?

X MARKS THE EMPTY GRAVE[1]

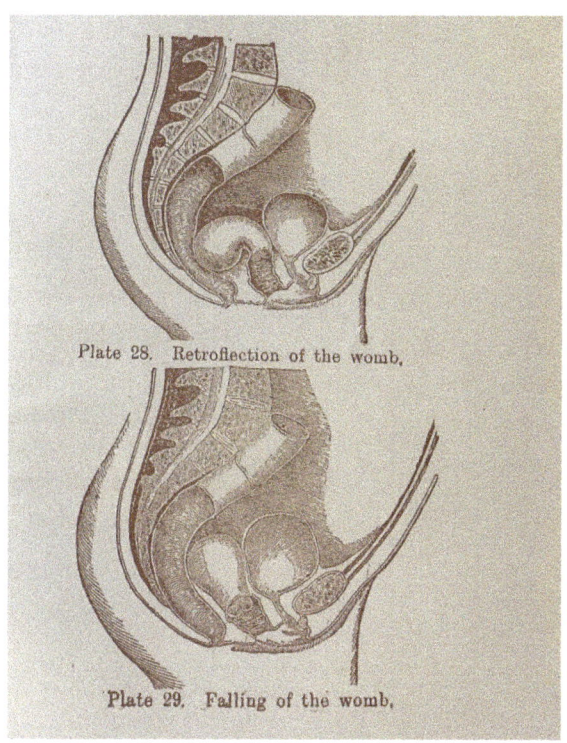

Plate 28. Retroflection of the womb.

Plate 29. Falling of the womb.

[1] Have you tried / to imagine

/ / emptiness / /

as something other / than a void?
Filled your map / with coordinates
to pretend / you have somewhere / to go?

Have you recognized / accepted
your body / was more   / / bilge / /
than sail?

EVEN THE AIR, TOO HEAVY

I held your
shape. Arms folded
across chest,
supported
your disappearance.
I woke
a heat in
my arms, a
cadenced desert
of smelted vanadium,
clapping cymbals clamoring
in desecrated wind.
My bones
lamented what I
would never hold.

ECHO

I hate beginning a new menstrual cycle, the throb up where it's tightest
and most warm. Not a
cramp, a reminder of one, the first breath of one,

a pinch, a gasp inside my cervix. Not pain and not pleasure, but both,
like the splintering of tree
bark after a man has thrust himself into me.

I feel this painful pinch, this punch, this pleasing splinter in the days
leading up to my menses,
carefully watching for blood.

I hate this feeling.

Reminds me of who I am not, of everything I cannot have in this temple
filled with echoes.
Echoes of no pregnancies,

echoes of pregnancies undone, unfinished, unraveled, unembedded,
echoes of their neverness,
their infinite and continuous fatality.

Echoes of me before the miscarriages, before the freezing boil, before the fantasy of pills.

I hate this feeling.

Reminds me of the echoes, builds echoes of echoes, points to the places where echoes echo
loudest.

I hate cramps confessing the truth of *no babies*, reminding me I don't want children, confessing I
will always want children.

I hate the pleasing pain that shakes the foundation of my cervical caverns, telling me the echoes
need somewhere to go, reminding me my blood is the river they used to escape.

No fetus in my wombless womb now, just thorns scraping at the places where my body most
betrayed me.

I hate this feeling.

These echoes that will always echo themselves echoing themselves
echoing this body
escaping itself

because

this body is the echo,
this body is the echo,
this body is the echo

SOURCES

Page 20, "Kinesthetic Alignment"
Page 33, "Spontaneous Abortion"
Page 42, "Wayward Winds"
Page 47, "X Marks the Empty Grave"

Descriptive Plates Illustrating the Female Reproductive Organs.
(Star Publishing Company, 1891)

Page 24, "Latitude & Longitude"

Kals, William S. *The Stargazer's Bible.* (Doubleday, 1980)

Page 6, "Through the Pores"
Page 15, "Division of the Fetus"
Pages 34-35, "We Disappear"

Maygrier, Jacque Pierre, et al. *Midwifery Illustrated.*
(Moore & Payne, 1833)

ACKNOWLEDGMENTS

Thank you to the literary journals who gave some of these poems
and their earlier drafts a place to belong:

Chasing Shadows for publishing my poems "Echo," "Pregnancy How-
Not-To Guide," and "I Cannot Carry these Fists" in their inaugural issue.

Silkworm for publishing my poem "Monument" in their literary journal.

Fox Paw Literary Blog for publishing my poem "Death Howler."

Other Worldly Women Press for publishing my poem "Grief."

Wingless Dreamer Publisher for publishing my poem "Butterfly Effect."

Enormous thank yous to those who have given my work consideration.
To everyone in the Sunday writing salon where most of these poems
were first written: Kate, Nan, Alex, Rebecca, Margaret, Sarah, Dee Ann,
Gail, Annette . . . your encouragement and support means absolutely
everything to me. I love you all.

To the peers who helped me revise this manuscript: Joanna, Brian,
Ocean, Manya . . . your feedback and reception of my poems kept me
going, even when I felt the subject of this book was insurmountable.
Thank you for holding such tender space for my work.

To the mentors who challenged, pushed, and believed in me over
the course of this manuscript's inception and revision: Vi Khi Nao,

Matt Hart, Alison C Rollins, Asiya Wadud, and Brandon Shimoda . . .
I will carry your support with me always.

To the teachers who encouraged my creative endeavors: Nicole
Roseveare, Ryan Davis, Carol Burnell, Sue Mach, Amanda Coffee,
Taylor Donnelly, Matthew Warren, Trevor Dodge, and everyone else
in the Clackamas Community College English Department, as well as
Jay Ponteri, Keri Behre, Meg Roland, and Perrin Kerns from Marylhurst
University . . . your encouragement lead me here. You changed my life.
Thank you for everything.

To so many of the friends who have loved and supported me through
this journey: Rachel, Cheryl, Molly, Angelee, Elaine, Christopher, Kasey,
Jessica, Erik, Russell, Adrianna, Leah . . . your friendship is a beacon of
light in my life, and your support fills me with gratitude. I love you all and
I am so very lucky to have you in my life.

To my soulmate, sister, and best friend in the entire world: Ashli . . .
you will always be my Legolas. I cherish you. I love you. I'm blessed to
hold you so close to my heart.

To my editors Emily Moon and Caroline Reul, and everyone at
First Matter Press . . . thank you a hundred lifetimes over for giving this,
my debut manuscript, a home.

To the other writers with *First Matter Press* who gave me feedback on
my work: Ahuva, Ash, Natalie, Sonja, Xylo . . . I can't express how much
I value your perspective, your suggestions, and the space you held for
this book. Thank you so much.

To my mom, who has always been my biggest fan; to my dad, who first
inspired me to love books, and to my brother, who always talks with me
about literature . . . I love you.

RILEY DANVERS is a bisexual poet living in Portland, Oregon with her partner, their cat, Lester, and corgi, Kiki. She graduated in 2016 with her A.S. in English and in 2018 with her B.A. in English Literature and Writing. Her fiction and nonfiction have been published in more than twenty-five online and printed literary journals and anthologies. Her poetry has been published in *Z Publishing House*, *Silkworm*, *Clackamas Literary Review*, *Other Worldly Women Press*, *Chasing Shadows*, and *Fox Paw Literary Blog*. Riley graduated with her M.F.A. in Creative Writing from Willamette University in 2021, and is currently pursuing a M.A. in Literature from Mercy College.

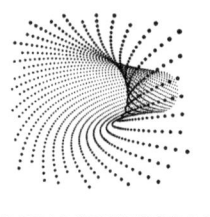

FIRSTMATTERPRESS
Portland, Ore.

First Matter Press is a collective press in Portland, Oregon, founded in 2018 to dissolve publication barriers for first-time publishing poets and genre-expanding writers. Our annual releases center community and craft by inviting authors into a creative cohort where they crystallize manuscripts in dialogue with editors and fellow writers and collaborate with featured artists on original cover art.

We are a 501(c)(3) non-profit organization and our authors maintain 100% copyrights and sales royalties of published work. Find our titles at IndieBound.org, Powells.com, BN.com and other major bookseller websites.

2022
FEATURED COVER ARTIST RACHEL MULDER

BETWEEN THESE BORDERS WANDERS A GOLEM
ahuva s. zaslavsky

EVEN THE AIR, TOO HEAVY
riley danvers

ONE ROW AFTER / BIR SIRA SONRA
sonya wohletz

SOMEONE I CAN HOLD GENTLY
xylophone mykland

STORIES FOR WHEN THE WOLVES ARRIVE
hailey spencer

FIRSTMATTERPRESS.ORG

www.ingramcontent.com/pod-product-compliance
Lightning Source LLC
Chambersburg PA
CBHW051646120626
46551CB00015B/2236